TWO LEFTS: THE COMPETITION FOR LEADERSHIP
OF LATIN AMERICA

Latin America underwent a stunning transformation in the 1980s. What Samuel

Huntington termed the "Third Wave" of democracy swept the region and ushered in an

era of representative democracy across a continent long notorious for repressive

authoritarian regimes.[1] Huntington noted that "In 1974 eight of ten South American

countries had nondemocratic governments."[2] By 1990 the opposite was true; all had

democratic governments except for Paraguay.[3] Many academics and U.S. foreign policy

experts exultantly proclaimed political success in the Americas. Francis Fukuyama even

went as far as proclaiming the supremacy of western democracy and the "End of

History."[4] And yet in time as the third wave receded, many Latin American nations

veered toward the left. Hugo Chavez Frias was the first in this new transformation of the

political landscape of Latin America with his election to the presidency of Venezuela in

1998. Chile (2000), Brazil (2002), Argentina (2003), Uruguay (2004), Bolivia (2005),

Ecuador (2006), Nicaragua (2006), Guatemala (2007), Paraguay (2008), El Salvador

(2009), and most recently Peru (2011) all followed suit and elected leftist presidents.[5]

History was alive again in Latin America.

But not all leftist presidents were the same. Some embraced a radical version of

populism, best exemplified by Hugo Chavez in Venezuela, while others adopted a more

moderate approach blending traditional leftist concerns for social justice with free

market economic policies as exemplified by Luiz Inacio "Lula" da Silva in Brazil. Yet

despite their many differences, Chavez and Lula shared one fundamental characteristic

– both deliberately set out to challenge, or if possible, replace U.S. hegemony in Latin

America. Sean Burgess wrote in 2007 that "Brazil and Venezuela are engaged in a contest for leadership of South America, each offering a different vision of how the regional geopolitical, geo-economic, and ideological space should be organized and directed."[6] This paper will explore the similarities and differences in the rise and trajectory of these two distinctly different "Lefts" in Latin America by examining Venezuela under Chavez and Brazil under Lula. The framework for this analysis will begin by defining radical populism and the moderate left. Next, each leader will be analyzed in turn by examining their rise to power, their social and economic policies, and the foreign policy trajectories they have undertaken. Finally, implications for U.S. policy in response to the regional leadership of Venezuela and Brazil will be given. Throughout the analysis this paper will seek to answer the following questions. Which of these models is most politically and economically sustainable and why? Which offers the best hope of prosperity and stability for its citizens? More importantly, will Brazil or Venezuela emerge as the regional leader of Latin America and if so, what are the implications for U.S. foreign policy?

Radical Populism and the Moderate Left Defined

In beginning to understand these two lefts it is useful to examine the underlying political models they are founded upon. Although there is a general consensus that Venezuela's Hugo Chavez is a populist, political scientists and international relations theorists disagree on the exact term that best describes his unique form of populism. "Hybrid Regime," "Contestatory Left," "Neo-populism" and "Radical Populism" have all been used to describe Chavez's political style.[7] An in-depth exploration of the nuanced differences between these various labels is outside the scope of this paper. For our purposes a general definition of populism and a focus on the Venezuelan model in

2

particular will suffice. In Latin America, populism is associated with a charismatic leader who unites previously marginalized socio-economic or labor groups with promises of jobs and social benefits and then mobilizes them to form a political power base.[8] Sebastian Edwards explains that,

> When defining *populism*, political theorists and historians usually refer to political movements led by individuals with strong and charismatic personalities whose attractiveness to the masses stems from a fiery rhetoric that centers on the causes and solutions to inequality. Their discourse pitches the interests of "the people" against those of the oligarchy, corporations, financial capital, the business sector and foreign companies.[9]

Chavez's version of populism, or *Chavismo,* is a modernized version which adds some unique aspects. Javier Corrales and Michael Penfold identified three additional traits of Chavismo; "a militaristic bent, state oriented economic policies, and a distinctive foreign policy that is committed to balancing the influence of the United States and exporting its radical political ideology across the region."[10] Another defining characteristic of *Chavismo* is how it deals with internal and external conflict. Chavez has embraced polarization as a powerful political tool for dealing with domestic and international conflict. Francisco Panizza explains that, "After starting his government as a moderate "Third Way" reformer, Chavez radicalized his positions and progressively expanded the political dividing line between himself and his enemies with attacks against neoliberalism and US imperialism that… came to represent not just his political enemies, but the enemies of the Venezuelan people."[11] In other words, Chavez successfully cast himself as the defender of the Venezuelan people. Internationally, Chavez sought to cast himself as the champion and defender of the left in Latin America, but with only mixed results.

In contrast to radical populism, the moderate left, as exemplified by Lula in Brazil, seeks to reform existing institutions rather than replacing them and strives for accommodation with its rivals in lieu of polarization. Under Lula's leadership, Brazil has adopted a modernized social democratic model. Social justice and economic redistribution remain core tenets of social democracy,[12] but as Brands notes, modern Latin American social democrats "now combine their traditional emphasis on social justice with responsible macroeconomic policies, respect for democratic procedures, and an aversion to polarizing practices and rhetoric."[13] In contrast to Chavez's personalistic form of regional leadership and efforts to spread his "twenty-first century socialism," Lula has sought to establish and expand Brazil's leadership both in Latin America and internationally as an emerging nation. Lula's goal was not to export a political model, but to secure markets and sustain Brazilian economic growth.

Hugo Chavez in Venezuela

In 1992, Lieutenant Colonel Hugo Chavez of the Venezuelan Army attempted to seize the presidency by force. He failed and spent the next two years in prison. However, his one-minute television address to the nation -- a precondition of his surrender to government forces -- made him a national celebrity.[14] Six years after his failed coup attempt Chavez won the presidency with 56 percent of the vote.[15] However, Chavez didn't win as an experienced political activist at the head of traditional party. Instead, he won as a political outsider riding a wave of voter discontent and apathy twenty years in the making.[16] As Gregory Wilpert vividly describes,

> Real per capita income suffered a massive and steady decline over a period of twenty years, from 1979 to 1999, declining by as much as 27% in this period. No other economy in South America experienced such a dramatic fall. Along with this drop, poverty increased, from 17% in 1980 to 65% in 1996... Eventually not enough resources were available to

4

maintain the clientelistic-corporatistic political culture, which then dealt a deadly blow to the two main political parties and enabled the rise and election a political outsider. Loyalty to the system had essentially been bought with hard cash rather than earned through political persuasion, so when the money ran out, so did the loyalty.[17]

George Philip observed the same phenomenon when we wrote that "the Punto Fijo system [the Venezuelan political power sharing arrangement in place since 1958[18]] was designed to be socially inclusive and to use oil money as a means of co-opting a whole range of social groups. The design worked adequately when the economy was progressing, but disastrously when (as happened from around 1981) the economy went into decline."[19] Chavez is widely credited with destroying the old political order in Venezuela, but he fully embraced the Venezuelan tradition of using oil revenue to generate political loyalty.[20]

Chavez began transforming the Venezuelan political and social landscape, in effect implementing his "Bolivarian Revolution," immediately following his inauguration in February 1999.[21] A key tenet of "Bolivarianism" would be the consolidation of presidential power. Soon after taking office Chavez called a referendum asking voters to support holding a new constituent assembly to draft a new constitution. Chavez won and a new constitution was enacted in 1999 which extended presidential terms to six years and allowed consecutive reelection for one term.[22] Chavez immediately ran for re-election under the provisions of the new constitution in 2000 and won, thereby resetting the clock on his term of office.[23]

Chavez next turned his attention to the Judiciary and Legislature. In May 2004 Chavez undermined the autonomy of the country's Supreme Court by expanding its membership from 20 to 32 and packing the new seats with his supporters.[24] The December 2005 National Assembly (Venezuela's legislative body) elections eliminated one of the last remaining checks on presidential power; when the opposition boycotted the elections in a bid to trigger international condemnation, Chavez was handed 100% control of the legislature.[25] As one author notes, "Following the 2005 election, Venezuela's National Assembly became a mere rubberstamp of presidential bills, rather than a bargaining actor."[26]

Chavez also sought to curtail the power and influence of other political actors in Venezuela. He purged opposition military officers and appointed "Chavista" officers without Congressional approval thereby eliminating the potential for dissent and expanding his political control over the military. Chavez also purged career diplomats and replaced them with political appointees.[27] This move eliminated another potential forum for dissent and reasserted Chavez's control over diplomacy and foreign policy.

Perhaps most importantly for Chavez's consolidation of presidential power and the future implementation of his social programs, he transformed the national oil company from an autonomous but state owned industry to an organization firmly under presidential control. Javier Corrales explains,

> He illegally fired key board members of the state-owned oil company, PDVSA, which produced a widespread labor and business strike, prompting Chavez to fire an additional twenty thousand staff, completely eroding the autonomy of the fattest milk cow in the entire country and the most profitable of Latin America's state-owned enterprises.[28]

The importance of this move in allowing Chavez the means to perpetuate himself in power is hard to understate. Venezuela is a petro-state; oil accounts for 95% of exports and 55% of government revenue.[29] All other sectors of the Venezuelan economy pale in comparison with oil. PDVSA contributed $38 billion in tax revenue in 2008 and $24.7 billion in 2009. Moreover, between 2004 and 2010 PDVSA contributed $61.4 billion to social development funds.[30] Windfall oil profits and exclusive oversight of government finances have given Chavez the means to buy political support domestically and internationally.

Since gaining office in 1999, Chavez has consistently sought to consolidate political power in the office of the president and undermine his political opposition. He has used oil revenues, political maneuvering and above all polarization in order to replace liberal democracy with his vision of "twenty-first-century socialism." Javier Corrales observed that,

> Politically, the Chavez regime changed Venezuela from a system in which incumbent and large opposition forces shared the spoils of office into a system of reduced political sharing... mostly because the executive branch has concentrated power, eroded the autonomy of checks and balances, reduced press freedoms, imposed costs on actors situated in the opposition....[31]

Corrales concludes that Chavez has in fact implemented a political revolution in Venezuela noting that, "Of all the elected governments in Latin America since the 1980s, not just those on the left, the Chavez administration has undermined liberal institutions of democracy the most, to the point where it makes sense to speak of a transition to some form of autocracy."[32] It is clear that Hugo Chavez has engineered a shocking rupture with the political past in Venezuela but what of his social programs? Do they represent an equally dramatic break with the past or only a marginal change?

Chavez began implementing sweeping changes to social programs during his first term in office. His Social and Economic Development Plan of 2001-2007 listed achieving social justice as its primary objective. The plan's three sub-objectives were intended to achieve it: the universalization of social rights; the reduction of the inequality of wealth, income and quality of life; and the appropriation of the public realm as a collective good.[33] Taken at face value, these appear to be admirable goals but what have Chavez's social programs actually achieved?

Chavez initially gained widespread praise for reducing poverty and inequality, improving access to medical care and reducing malnutrition among Venezuela's urban poor. In 2007, Gregory Wilpert wrote that, "In the course of Chavez's presidency, from 1999 to 2006, the government made significant strides in redistributing wealth, via the land reform programs and social policies..."[34] Francisco Rodriguez, Chief Economist of the Venezuelan National Assembly from 2000-2004, stated "...just about everyone appears to agree that, in contrast to his predecessors, Chavez has made the welfare of the Venezuelan poor his top priority."[35] However, recent scholarship – much of it influenced by independent analysis conducted by Rodriguez – has taken a much more critical view. As Francisco Panizza notes,

> Chavez's Bolivarian Revolution has polarized not just the Venezuelan people, but also scholarly opinion about the nature of his regime. For his supporters he has radically democratized Venezuelan society, improving the lot of the poor, giving voice to the excluded and promoting direct democracy from below. For his opponents, he is an elected autocrat who has destroyed liberal democracy and used the country's oil wealth to promote a megalomaniac project of personalistic rule.[36]

Panizza's cites statistics showing that poverty in Venezuela fell from over 50 percent in 1999 to between 42 percent and 33 percent by 2007.[37] Rodriguez cites the decline in poverty from 54 percent in 2003 to 27.5 percent in the first half of 2007.[38] However, Rodriguez also notes that, "Although this decline may appear impressive, it is also known that poverty reduction is strongly associated with economic growth and that Venezuela's per capita GDP grew by nearly 50 percent during the same period – thanks in great part to a tripling of oil prices."[39] Both authors agree that contrary to perceptions, the proportion of government spending Chavez has allocated to social programs is basically unchanged from that of previous governments. Rodriguez notes that social

programs under Chavez averaged 25.12 percent of budget outlays in his first eight

years in office, almost no change from the 25.08 percent average in the eight years

prior to his election in 1998.[40] Javier Corrales concludes that, "the claim that Chavez's

overall social spending represents a break with the past is overstated. …There is more

spending simply because Chavez enjoyed the largest inflow of revenue in Venezuela

since the 1930s."[41] Setting aside the issue of whether Chavez has spent more or less

on social programs than previous governments, what has he achieved with his

spending?

In his generally sympathetic analysis of Chavez's twenty-first-century socialism,

Gregory Wilpert identifies three characteristics that represent a break from previous

governments. First he cites "a tremendous increase" in social spending on redistributive

programs such as free education and health care, subsidized food and housing, and

rural and urban land reform.[42] Next he notes that Chavez bypassed existing government

institutions and created new organizations – his "*missiones*" or missions concept – to

implement his social programs. Lastly, Chavez enlisted local communities in the

"missions" process. As Wilpert explains, "This citizen participation has proved to

contribute significantly to mobilizing the population both in defense of the social

programs and in defense of the government…"[43] A critical analysis of these three

"revolutionary" aspects of Chavez's social policy identifies two outcomes that help

explain why Chavez chooses to fund them. First his redistributive programs, while they

may help alleviate some pressure of poverty, are not formulated to eradicate it. These

policies create dependencies on government handouts and subsidies rather than creating development. However, they do generate an effect that the last two characteristics share; they create a pool of "clients" who receive benefits from the state and in return they are expected to support the state (Chavez) with their votes.

Creating parallel state institutions (the missions) and enlisting local committees also helped to create a vast new pool of clients. This is not to argue that Chavez has not helped the poor – he has; the question is to what end. As Corrales and Penfold note,

> Although some programs were influenced by poverty considerations, most programs were used to buy votes at the municipal level. As a consequence, clientelism and poverty spending interacted closely. In fact, in the act of distributing cash, the Chavez regime was able to simultaneously "buy votes" while distributing oil income to the very poor.[44]

The net benefit to Chavez is perpetuation in office. The effect on Venezuelan democracy is decidedly negative; the mechanism for presidential transitions has been suppressed. As Corrales and Penfold conclude,

> The key point is that a combination of opportunistic social spending and declining accountability has decisive political effects: on the one hand, it fosters clientelism; on the other it perhaps leads to an administration that is virtually impossible to defeat electorally. The opposition can never match the level of resources deployed by the state... Spending has given the Chavez regime an advantage in competing for votes: his government competes with words and money, the opposition, with words only.[45]

Chavez has built a vast system of patronage based on creating "clients" that support him politically in return for government jobs and social programs funded by Venezuela's oil wealth. He has also successfully subverted democracy at home by eliminating, suppressing or co-opting other political actors (the military, legislature and judiciary), consolidating presidential power and eliminating term limits. With a consolidated base of power at home and the prospect of many years in office, how has Chavez interacted on the regional and international stage?

Chavez's foreign policy also represents a radical break with the past – and like his domestic and social policies it has generated intense polarization. Chavez listed five foreign policy objectives for his government in its 2001-2007 National Development Plan: "promote multi-polarity, promote Latin American integration, consolidate and diversify Venezuela's international relations, strengthen Venezuela's position in the international economy, and promote a new regime of hemispheric security."[46] Although these objectives seem benign, Chavez's actual foreign policy actions have been much more divisive and at times even counterproductive. The two most salient features of Chavez's vision of multi-polarity entail opposing U.S. regional and international hegemony and using Venezuela's oil wealth to support the spread of leftist governments in Latin America.

Historically, Venezuela had been a staunch ally of the United States and a regional promoter of democracy and reconciliation. The change in relations after Chavez's election was dramatic and swift. As Javier Corrales and Michael Penfold succinctly observed,

> Under Chavez, Venezuela changed direction. Vis-á-vis the United States, Venezuela became the most uncooperative country in the region after Cuba and a strident critic of almost every U.S foreign policy initiative. Vis-á-vis other Latin American countries, Caracas started to emphasize close ties with social movements and political leaders seeking "revolutionary" change, rather than political conciliation and gradual reforms... the level of tension and decline of cooperation in U.S.-Venezuela relations are without precedent.[47]

Beyond simply resisting U.S. hegemony, Chavez has sought to actively oppose U.S. interests – by implementing "soft balancing."

Corrales and Penfold define soft balancing as "efforts by nations to *frustrate* the foreign policy objectives of other, presumably more powerful nations, but stopping short

11

of military actions."[48] While acknowledging that not all of Chavez's actions fit the model exactly, the authors do cite specific examples of Venezuelan soft balancing:[49]

- Systematically eschewing cooperation, for example, on drug interdiction and security

- Building alliances with other like-minded nations, such as Iraq prior to the U.S. invasion, Iran Libya, Cuba, Syria, Byelorussia, and Zimbabwe

- Creating obstacles in international forums, for example, organizing an anti-U.S. parallel Summit of the Americas in 2005

- Promoting counterproposals such as launching in 2006 the "Bolivarian alternative" to Free Trade in the Americas (ALBA), a trade agreement that opposes trade liberalization and privatization [includes Venezuela, Bolivia, Cuba and Nicaragua]

- Generating diplomatic entanglements, such as discussing with Russia the installation of military bases and deployment of missiles in either Cuba or Venezuela; intruding in negotiations between Bogota and the FARC

- Openly accusing the United States of posing an economic and military national threat to the revolution; or of planning to assassinate Chavez or invade the country from Colombia, Aruba, or Costa Rica; and ordering the military to prepare for "asymmetrical war" against imperialism

Soft balancing has impeded some U.S foreign policy efforts but it has also polarized regional and international opinions of Chavez.

A second pillar of Chavez's foreign policy is the export of social programs and oil subsidies to generate what Corrales and Penfold have labeled "social power diplomacy."[50] They note that, "Venezuela under Chavez has become a world champion of foreign aid" funding social projects in Nicaragua, Cuba, Argentina, Ecuador, Honduras, Peru and Bolivia. Chavez has also subsidized oil exports to Cuba and several Caribbean and Central American nations; provided cash handouts to Bolivia, and financed the Argentine government by buying $1.3 billion dollars in bonds after it defaulted on its international debt in 2001.[51] Chavez has also funded populist candidates in Mexico, Peru, Nicaragua, Ecuador and Bolivia.[52] He triggered a scandal in

2007 when a Venezuelan-U.S. businessman was arrested in Buenos Aires carrying

$800,000 in undeclared funds to finance Christina Fernandez de Kirchner's election

campaign.[53]

While Corrales and Penfold note that "few other countries compare with Venezuela

in deploying social power" they caution that "in reality, however, Venezuela's social

power diplomacy has little to do with social development."[54]

> Venezuela has not focused on the export of guerilla war, as Cuba did
> during the cold war, nor on the export of weapons, as Russia still does.
> Via its aid and business deals, Venezuela has exported a particular form
> of corruption. Billed as investments in social services, it in fact consisted
> largely of unaccountable financing for political campaigns, unelected
> social movements, business deals, and political patronage by state
> officials.[55]

If Chavez's foreign investments do not generate development then what is their

purpose and what does Chavez gain? Beyond seeking to generate soft power to

balance the aid and development programs of the United States, Corrales and Penfold

offer another explanation:

> A hybrid regime [Chavez's government] operating on a continent with so
> many democracies faces a particular foreign policy challenge: being
> ostracized and admonished by neighboring states. This situation compels
> the hybrid regime to make an extra effort to neutralize potential sources of
> criticism and even win over neighbors as allies. One way to do this is to
> give lavish foreign aid. Precisely because Latin America is predominantly
> democratic, Chavez must invest heavily in efforts to inhibit expressions of
> concern and to preempt rebukes coming from these countries with gifts.
> Moreover, to effectively buy the silence or non-censure of social
> progressives abroad, this foreign aid must adopt the veneer of progressive
> values.[56]

Thus Chavez operates in a cycle of influence peddling; he relies on political polarization

and fiery rhetoric to motivate his political base and espouse his socialist revolution, but in order to deflect criticism (and create the perception of support) Chavez has to fund foreign aid programs and finance leftist politicians abroad.

Luiz Inacio "Lula" da Silva in Brazil

In 2002 some 60 percent of Brazilian voters cast their ballots for Luiz Inacio "Lula" da Silva to be their next president.[57] Far from a political outsider like Chavez, Lula rose to the presidency of Brazil at the head of a traditional political party and only after many years of campaigning; his 2002 win came on his third bid for the presidency.[58] Wendy Hunter noted that, "Lula's victory meant that, for the first time in Brazil's history, a highly organized party with a sense of ideological purpose and deep roots in society would head the government."[59] Yet international investors and political analysts worried that Lula might also implement a form of populism and steer Brazil hard to the left. Their worries were not unfounded.

Lula, a former union leader, and his *Partido dos Trabalhadores* (Worker's Party or PT) had long advocated nationalization of privately owned companies and redistribution of land among other policies.[60] Peter Kingstone and Aldo Ponce noted that, "For observers on Wall Street, the election of a one-time Socialist and seemingly dedicated leftist president raised concerns about Lula da Silva's commitment to the market oriented reforms and financial stability achieved by his predecessor..."[61] Would Lula follow in Chavez's footsteps and seek a radical break with the past in Brazil or would he chart his own course?

Lula's own actions best define his interpretation of the moderate left. From the beginning of his presidency, Lula charted a course nearly opposite that of Chavez. As will be described in greater detail in the sections that follow, Lula has developed three defining characteristics of the moderate left: reform over revolution, gradual

14

improvement instead of radical change and multilateralism over ideology. In both domestic and foreign policies, Lula has consistently sought reform over revolutionary change – improve existing structures and organizations instead of replacing them. Lula has consistently chosen gradual improvement over rapid, radical change. And finally, Lula has sought not to export an ideology, but rather to promote multilateralism on the world stage and South American integration at home – both of which seek to create space for the growth of Brazilian markets and the expansion of trading partners. How then has Lula implemented these principals in his political, economic and social policies?

One insight into Lula's political policies as president can be gleaned from the manner in which he achieved office. Unlike Chavez, the one-time coup leader, Lula da Silva has shown a steadfast commitment to the democratic "rules of the game." Francisco Panizza noted that, "In contrast to the Venezuelan president's progressive political radicalization, Lula da Silva has travelled an opposite path, from radicalism to moderation."[62] In this Lula reflected the personality of his party. Panizza concludes that "The PT was never a revolutionary party, and its radical rhetoric was always tempered with a respect for the democratic rules of the game and a considerable dose of pragmatism."[63] So when looking backwards it comes as no surprise to find that Lula continued to work within the existing political and party system despite very close electoral defeats in 1989 and 1994.[64] Also not surprising is the fact that Lula carried this respect for democracy forward with him into office.

Perhaps most important is what the literature does not say about Lula. The research conducted for this paper did not identify a single instance of Lula seeking to modify the structure of the Brazilian government to expand presidential power, extend presidential term limits or change the constitution to perpetuate himself in power. Lula's most definitive commitment to democracy came in January 2011 when he passed the office of the presidency to fellow PT party candidate Dilma Rousseff.[65] A defining characteristic of the moderate left is working within the existing framework of democracy instead of seeking a radical change in government structure and the balance of power. It is also a key political difference between Lula and Chavez; Lula worked for change within the existing system, while Chavez sought to replace the existing system with one more to his liking. What then of Lula's economic and social policies? Did Lula seize control of the sources of government revenue to fund his social programs as Chavez did in Venezuela?

Rather than seeking to implement radical change and a dismantling of Brazilian capitalism, Lula once again sought moderation and incremental improvement to existing policies and structures. Sebastian Edwards sums it up when he writes that, "President Lula surprised pundits and experts of all stripes by strictly avoiding the populist temptation. During his tenure Brazil has shown strict respect for property rights and as a result has attracted large volumes of direct foreign investment."[66] Kingstone and Ponce similarly noted that,

> Lula's success is not a reflection of a sharp break with the past and an inversion of priorities. Instead he benefited from an unusually positive international economy until 2008, and by maintaining continuity with the policies and policy orientations of his predecessor...[67]

Kingstone and Ponce go on to cite three tenets of Lula's economic orientation: monetary stability, flexibility in seeking market reform and a commitment to address poverty and inequality.[68] They further noted that,

These policies have helped Brazil achieve stability, modest growth, and a steady, gradualist commitment to addressing historic injustices. Some might argue that this is not a spectacular achievement, and there is no question that it leaves many important issues unresolved. But it is a considerable achievement given Brazil's turbulent history, and it lays the groundwork for continued gradual improvement.[69]

"Gradual improvement" could well serve as the bumper sticker for Lula's tenure as president of Brazil. It defines his version of the moderate left approach in almost every area of governance and serves as a vivid counterpoint to Chavez's model of polarization and radical change. What about Lula's social programs – what has gradual improvement achieved and is the pace fast enough to avoid more radical solutions?

In counterpoint to Chavez's extensive spending of oil income on redistributive social programs to address inequality and poverty (and to buy votes), Lula relied primarily on growing the Brazilian economy to ameliorate poverty. Brazilian Finance Minister, Antonio Palocci, summed it up when he said that, "enhancing the welfare of poor Brazilians would depend first on maintaining economic stability and achieving growth."[70] Kingstone and Ponce noted that "Lula's administration has consistently limited social expenditures in order to maintain its main priorities: macroeconomic balance and low inflation rates."[71] Lula's macroeconomic approach did achieve some notable success; unemployment fell from 12.3% in 2003 to 7.9% in 2008 and he showed a slight increase in social spending - to 22.4% of GDP per capita - up from 20.7% under his predecessor.[72]

Beyond a reliance on macroeconomic policies to generate economic improvement for all Brazilians, Lula also reorganized and expanded Brazil's existing social programs. In describing Lula's social programs Wendy Hunter observed that,

> While shying away from redistributive reforms that would have challenged property and privilege, the PT-led government made advances in social

17

assistance... The conditional cash transfer program *Bolsa Família* comprised the social policy centerpiece of Lula's presidency. Operating squarely within existing fiscal and political boundaries, it provided minimal social protection to the poor without threatening more expensive well-established social programs enjoyed by the middle and upper classes.[73]

One of Lula's most successful efforts was the expansion of an innovative cash transfer program for poor families. Lula created Bolsa Família in 2003 by combining four pre-existing poverty programs and developing a single national registry of poor families.[74] Bolsa Família is both targeted and conditional; families with monthly income below minimum wage are eligible for enrollment but in order to receive cash transfers all children in the family must attend school and receive basic health care.[75] Sebastian Edwards cites a recent World Bank study:

> The virtue of Bolsa Família is that it reaches a significant portion of Brazilian society that has never benefited from social programs. It is among the world's best targeted programs, because it reaches those who really need it. Ninety-four percent of the funds reach the poorest 40 percent of the population. Studies prove that most of the money is used to buy food, school supplies, and clothes for the children. [76]

Beyond improving the functionality of the transfer programs, Lula also greatly increased their scope. Participation in the Bolsa Família program ballooned from 3.6 million in 2003 to over 11 million by 2006.[77] The program also generated soft power benefits for Brazil; similar programs have been implemented in Mexico, Colombia, Honduras and Nicaragua.[78]

However, Lula's social policies were not popular with all of segments of the PT party. Many party loyalists thought Lula's programs did not go far enough; some criticized *Bolsa Família* as a handout program with one PT deputy going as far as saying, "We didn't struggle for two decades in the opposition for this!"[79] Despite resistance from more radical elements within the PT, Lula's macroeconomic approach did bear fruit. Sebastian Edwards noted that,

> In spite of criticism from his own supporters who wanted to favor income distribution over price stability and growth, Lula persevered... With inflation under control and reduced overall economic instability, consumer credit soared, and for the first time in a generation the lower middle class and the poor had widespread access to white goods, vacations and automobiles and, perhaps more important, could obtain mortgages and become homeowners.[80]

Kingstone and Ponce agreed noting that, "The reduction in poverty (at an annual average of 7.9% between 2003-2007) seems to stem from Brazil's moderate economic growth... and from a large increase in the number of beneficiaries of Brazil's innovative income transfer programs, particularly the conditional cash transfers associated with the Bolsa Família."[81]

However, Bolsa Família is not perfect. Echoing Wendy Hunter's observation above that the program is an incremental change and not true social reform, Kingstone and Ponce observed that the program is not a significant increase in social spending and therefore "is less promising with respect to creating fundamental changes in Brazil's social and economic structure."[82] Regardless of internal PT party debates or concerns about the long term efficacy of Bolsa Família, the program did contribute to Lula's popularity. Sebastian Edwards notes that "Bolsa Família is very popular with the people. Indeed, many analysts credit it for Lula's very high approval rating and his easy reelection to the presidency in 2006."[83] Like Bolsa Família, Lula's first term was not perfect. In fact Lula's campaign for reelection labored under the burden of several corruption scandals.

Lula's willingness to sacrifice honesty for political expediency also generated criticism. Unlike Chavez who was willing to completely undermine democracy to achieve his goals, Lula was only willing to bend it a little – or at least look the other while his supporters did the dirty work. Kingstone and Ponce observe that,

> The radical left undermines existing institutions and democratic procedures to advance its political and economic program. By contrast, the moderate left is more oriented to negotiation with the opposition and is willing to make concessions to preserve the institutional and procedural aspects of democratic governance.[84]

As discussed above, Chavez used Venezuela's vast oil wealth to create new forms of patronage and to in effect buy votes at the local level while subordinating the other branches of government to the presidency. Lula's supporters implemented a more targeted approach. They bypassed the electorate and went beyond concessions to the opposition to gain supporters for his policies. Instead of modifying the system, Lula's supporters simply began paying opposition congressmen a monthly payment of approximately $12,000 USD in return for their votes.[85] The ensuing scandal rocked Brazilian politics and led to the downfall of some of Lula's closest allies, but it did not prevent his reelection in 2006.[86] Did Lula's foreign policy follow the same model of reform over revolution and a preference for gradual improvement? Have Lula's foreign policy efforts garnered a similar level of success or have they also generated mixed results and controversy?

Regionally, Brazil renewed its efforts to establish regional leadership and achieved some notable successes in its efforts to promote South American integration. Brazil helped block the United States initiative to establish the Free Trade Area of the Americas (FTAA), advocating in its place for greater continental, as opposed to hemispheric, integration.[87] In counterpoint to FTAA, Brazil sought to reinvigorate the Southern Common Market (MERCOSUR) and pursued a long-term vision of regional integration loosely modeled on the European Union.[88] This effort came to fruition in

2008 when twelve South American nations signed a formal treaty establishing the Union

of South American States (UNASUR). Riordan Roett noted,

> Brazil's leadership role in the UNASUR initiative has been critical. As the acknowledged leader in South American regional efforts (reluctantly accepted by President Hugo Chavez of Venezuela who has, in the past, hoped that his country would play the role), the government of President Lula has taken a broad historical vision of the goal of deeper regional integration.[89]

Lula has implemented a similar policy of integration, multilateralism and expanding

Brazilian leadership at the global level.

Under Lula's leadership Brazil has taken historic steps to move out onto the

world stage. Brazil's rising economic and political clout allowed Lula to flex new-found

muscle in the international economic, diplomatic and military spheres. In her *Foreign

Affairs* article Julia Sweig observed that, "unlike Chavez, who distributes his country's

petro-largess for explicitly political and ideological purposes, Brazil has translated its

investments and economic prowess in Latin America into influence on the global

stage."[90] Brazil has also set its sights higher than Chavez – rather than seek twenty-first-

century socialism in Latin America, Lula is seeking a new multilateralism in world affairs

and a greater international role for Brazil. As with his domestic policies, Lula has shown

a strong commitment to the international "rules of the game" but also willingness to

attempt an unconventional approach in selected circumstances. Brazil has increased its

international presence under Lula, but there have also been setbacks along the way.

International trade policy stands as one of the hallmarks of Lula's foreign

relations efforts. Brazil has sought greater South-South (Southern hemisphere)

integration internationally and has positioned itself as a leader among developing

nations. Brazil assumed the mantle of championing the rights of developing nations in

2003 when it played a key role in expanding the Group of Seven industrialized members of the World Trade Organization into the Group of 20 or G20 which now includes prominent developing nations. Brasilia also established new South-South linkages such as the India-Brazil-South Africa Dialogue Forum (IBSA).[91] And of course most famously, Brazil is a charter member of the BRICs (Brazil, Russia, India and China) -- four countries identified by Goldman Sachs in 2001 as rising economic powers.[92] Although the BRICs have not achieved a fundamental reorganization of international financial and political institutions, they have undeniably gained a strong voice and they can exert considerable influence when their interests align. Brazil is also a founding member of the United Nations and has served ten rotational terms as a member of the Security Council. However, in one of his bitterest setbacks Lula ultimately failed in his efforts to reform the Security Council and gain a permanent Brazilian seat.[93]

On a brighter note, Lula achieved greater success in expanding the international prestige and reputation of his armed forces. Brazil sought and assumed the leadership of the United Nations Stabilization Mission in Haiti (MINUSTAH) in 2004 – a mission they continue to lead – after Haitian President Jean-Bertrand Aristide fled the country amid an atmosphere of lawlessness and chaos.[94] The U.S. welcomed Brazilian leadership of MINUSTAH; American forces were fully engaged in combat operations in Afghanistan and Iraq with little desire to add a stability mission to their slate of global operations, even if Haiti does lie just off the U.S. mainland. The Brazilian government and military have proven their leadership and resiliency in a challenging overseas assignment, their first major operation since the Dominican Republic in 1965, by weathering the suicide of a force commander and the devastating earthquake that struck Port au Prince in

January 2010.[95] Regionally and internationally, Brazil has proven it can lead complex multinational operations and overcome adversity without compromising the military mission or losing its domestic political will. Brazil has also gained credibility and prestige with regional partners serving in MINUSTAH – and gained valuable political and military experience.

However, not all has been sunshine and roses as Brazil exerted its fledgling international clout. Lula's most significant foreign policy setback came in his diplomatic efforts to broker a negotiated settlement of Iran's nuclear disagreements with the West. President Mahmud Ahmadinejad visited Brasilia in late 2009 along with stops in Venezuela and Bolivia. During the visit, "Lula affirmed Brazil's support for Iran's right to a civilian nuclear program and criticized attempts to isolate Iran over its nuclear ambitions. Lula said he opposed sanctions that had been threatened by the industrial countries and the United Nations and supported diplomacy."[96] Lula's position generated a domestic and international backlash.[97] As Julia Sweig notes, "Lula and Foreign Minister Celso Amorim's two-year initiative to broker an alternative to UN sanctions against Iran was perhaps the single most controversial - and, to some, most inexplicable – example of the new Brazil's international ambition.[98] Why would Lula seek to entangle Brazil with Iran and what did he hope to gain?

A variety of authors have posited an assortment of reasons for Lula's efforts to recognize Iran and his hope to broker a diplomatic settlement of Iran's nuclear issue. Riordan Roett cited the growth in Brazilian trade with Iran – which increased almost 100 percent between 2003 and 2007 to nearly $2 billion annually – along with a desire for Iranian support in its quest to secure a permanent Security Council seat.[99] The independent geopolitical analysis company STRATFOR posited independence from the U.S. as a possible motive when it wrote,

> Many Brazilians have no idea why the government is engaging abroad when it has no threats to face. But in its attempt to engage all comers – from the United States and Israel to Venezuela and Iran – Brazil acquires a reputation of neutrality by showing that it does not intend to subordinate its interests to those of the States.[100]

Julia Sweig provided another possible rationale; future economic gain. "Brazil is home to world's sixth-largest proven reserves of uranium," Sweig noted, "and by 2015… Brazil will possess an independent enrichment capability that could allow it to begin exporting enriched uranium." Sweig then concluded that, "Opposing sanctions against Iran – indeed, persuading it, at least in principle, to send its fuel abroad for enrichment under the International Atomic Energy Agency's watch – may well have been about preserving a market."[101]

Regardless of the motives, the diplomatic effort failed, damaging Lula's image and tarnishing Brazilian prestige. It remains unclear whether the episode was an example of diplomatic overreach or foreign policy naiveté. In either case, Brazil learned from the experience and has since stepped back from relations with Iran – President Mahmoud Ahmadinejad's 2012 visit to South America included Venezuela, Ecuador, Nicaragua and Cuba – but not Brazil.[102]

Implications for U.S. Security Policy: Venezuela

As with most issues surrounding Chavez, analysts and scholars hold opposing views of how his brand of radical populism affects U.S. security policy. Political idealists see Chavismo as a threat to democracy, stability and regional cooperation. As Hal Brands explains,

The revival of radical populism poses two principal challenges for U.S. policymakers. The first pertains to prospects for democratic stability and sustainable economic development in the region. The second has to do with hemispheric security and diplomatic cooperation and the overall tenor of U.S.-Latin American affairs.[103]

As shown previously, Chavez has undermined Venezuelan democracy by eliminating governmental checks and balances (through co-opting or suppressing other political actors), consolidating extraordinary presidential power and eliminating term limits. He has also chosen dependency over economic development by creating a patronage network funded by oil revenues. These actions run counter to the U.S. goals of supporting and spreading democracy but in the end, the Venezuelan electorate determines under which form of government the country lives.

Chavez's efforts to expand his influence and impede U.S. policy objectives across the region are more troublesome. He has created a loose anti-American alliance centered on the Bolivarian Alternative for the Americas (ALBA) nations: Venezuela, Bolivia, Cuba and Nicaragua. Together, these nations have undermined U.S. regional counter-drug, security and free trade goals, at least within their respective nations. Russell Crandall echoes the idealist viewpoint when he writes,

> No one should underestimate the capacity of the Venezuela-led block of quasi-authoritarian leftist governments to stop the regional trend toward greater openness and democracy – values the block sees representing a capitulation to the U.S.-controlled global system.[104]

However, there is a growing consensus that Chavez has passed the apogee of his regional appeal. As early as 2007, Chavez's abrasive rhetoric and aggressive style had eroded his popularity. In a regional opinion poll conducted that year Chavez earned the dubious distinction of being one of the most "widely mistrusted" world leaders.[105] Another author cited a Brazilian official who confided that, "the first thing that Brazil and a number of other countries try to do at inter-American meetings is marginalize the Venezuelan representative.[106]

While the ALBA nations will likely continue to at least nominally support Chavez and oppose U.S. regional goals, few other nations seek to join them. Corrales and Penfold note that,

> ...social-power diplomacy has not led to a realization of Chavez's grandiose visions for a paradigm shift in Latin America. It has not given rise to a massive coalition of Latin American nations against the United States... Few Latin American politicians now running for office want to be openly associated with Chavez.[107]

Chavez and his ALBA allies may be able to frustrate, or at least impede, U.S. regional goals on certain issues but the problem is manageable; U.S. policymakers and diplomats can negotiate these challenges in the future as they have over the last decade.

Political realists take a much narrower view of the challenge Chavez poses for the U.S. In their assessment, Venezuela is only important in terms of oil and oil is "the sole reason Venezuela has risen to the level of being geopolitically important."[108] In a 2006 analysis, STRATFOR's was even blunter:

> Washington ultimately doesn't care what Chavez does as long as he continues to ship oil to the United States. From the American point of view, Chavez – like Castro – is simply a nuisance, not a serious threat.[109]

While partially true, STRATFOR overstates the solitary importance of oil in U.S.-Venezuelan relations. Oil matters, but democracy and regional stability are also important. The U.S. does need to worry about Venezuelan oil, but not a decision by Chavez to stop exports. He will continue sending oil to the U.S. as long as Venezuela has oil to ship; has no other recourse. Chavez cannot stop exporting oil to the U.S. and continue to fund his patronage system and despite all his rhetoric and threats against

26

the U.S., Chavez never once stopped exporting oil to the United States during his fourteen years in office.[110] He also cannot easily shift his oil export to new markets; over fifty-percent of Venezuelan petroleum flows to the U.S. and the country remains reliant on U.S. refineries to process its distinctive product.[111] Corrales and Penfold explain,

> Venezuela's crude oil cannot be placed easily outside the United States: heavy and impure, with high sulfur content, it requires expressly built refineries found mainly in the United States. No other country has both the large energy needs and the refining capacity to process heavy crudes to absorb the bulk of Venezuelan oil.[112]

Nevertheless, a potential long-term concern for U.S. policymakers is the fact that Venezuela's oil production is in decline. Francisco Rodriguez notes that, "Production has been steadily declining since the government consolidated its control of the industry in late 2004. According to OPEC statistics, Venezuela currently produces only three-quarters of its quota of 3.3 million barrels a day."[113] Yet the critical future issue for U.S. policymakers is not an intentional disruption in Venezuelan oil exports or a decreasing production, instead they should worry about Venezuela's internal stability.

Chavez has built an empire based on oil revenues and his personal leadership. The loss or prolonged interruption of either would dramatically undermine Venezuelan stability. On the oil front, Chavez faces decreasing oil revenues due to falling prices and declining production. The loss of revenue is destabilizing for a populist government reliant on oil money to keep its project afloat. As STRATFOR observes,

> Despite government officials' avowals, it is only a matter of time before Caracas will have to start cutting back on social spending and raising taxes. This means hardship for Venezuelans who rely on the government to sustain subsidies and run national companies – and hardships for Venezuelans could mean destabilizing unrest for the country as a whole.[114]

STRATFOR's analysis is prescient and mirrors Venezuelan history. This same mechanism of rising discontent triggered by an interruption of the normal flow of patronage is what allowed Chavez to rise to power. Gregory Wilpert's description of the fall of the Punto Fijo system prior to Chavez could serve as the epitaph for Chavismo in the not too distant future, "Loyalty to the system had essentially been bought with hard cash rather than earned through political persuasion, so when the money ran out, so did the loyalty."[115]

Chavismo, and Venezuelan stability, face yet another destabilizing factor, the potential loss of Hugo Chavez. Cuban doctors diagnosed Chavez with prostate cancer in early 2011 and a January 24, 2012 CNN article reported that Chavez's cancer had spread to his colon, spine and bones.[116] The same article mentioned that Chavez may only have nine months left to live. Given the stakes, and the level political polarization ingrained over the last fourteen years, competition for control of the Venezuelan government if Chavez dies or is unable to continue in office is likely to be fierce and possibly bloody. STRATFOR notes that, "Serious factional divisions within the Chavista elite portend a real threat of violence... No individual exists right now with the leadership qualities to match Chavez."[117] Beyond violence within the Chavista movement, Venezuela also faces the very real potential for violence as the long-downtrodden opposition seeks to regain power after Chavez's fall. In either case, the potential for widespread instability – and a potential disruption of oil exports – would be very high.[118]

Venezuela presents U.S. policymakers with several challenges: how to deal with Chavez in office, what to do when Chavez eventually leaves power, and finally, how to reestablish positive relations with a post-Chavez Venezuela. The first scenario generates much debate but is actually rather simple; U.S. policymakers should maintain the current policy of "selective containment" as long as Chavez remains in office. Selective containment only engages Chavez on discrete issues of significant importance to U.S. interests such as condemning Venezuela's indifference to drug trafficking or its support of the Revolutionary Armed Forces of Colombia (FARC). Selective containment does not respond to Chavez's internal policies or his bombastic rhetoric.

How to respond if Chavez abruptly leaves office due to incapacity, death or his overthrow (by coup or electoral defeat) presents a greater challenge and U.S. policy options will be limited. The polarization of Venezuelan society and the politicization of the Venezuelan military make a smooth transition of power unlikely; a serious crisis, possibly leading to widespread instability is a more likely outcome. Any direct, overt U.S. participation in political or military responses to such a crisis would trigger a negative, and perhaps violent, backlash from Chavez's supporters. The U.S. would need to tread lightly in any post-Chavez response scenario and should seek to foster multilateral regional responses rather than rely on U.S.-led initiatives.

In the longer term, the U.S. faces a different challenge; how to reincorporate post-Chavez Venezuela into the political and security framework of the region. Reestablishing relations and rebuilding trust will take many years. Chavez has carefully crafted and nurtured political polarization and anti-Americanism in Venezuelan politics and society over the last thirteen years and those sentiments will not be quickly overcome. Nevertheless, relations can be repaired and the United States and Venezuela can regain their formerly close bilateral relationship, but it will take years of concerted effort by both parties. One of the first steps should be encouraging

Venezuelan participation in regional political and security forums that were shunned by

Chavez such the Organization of the American States and U.S.-sponsored regional

security exercises such as the annual Central American and Caribbean disaster

response exercise *Fuerzas Aliadas Humanitarias* (FA-HUM). Multilateral fora provide a

mechanism to reestablish official and interpersonal relationships between U.S. officials

and their Venezuelan counterparts. Over time, the U.S. can seek to reestablish bilateral

visits and working groups, encourage renewed Venezuelan attendance at U.S. military

schools, and seek other mutual acceptable confidence building measures.

Implications for U.S. Security Policy: Brazil

The United States faces a very different set of policy challenges regarding Brazil.

In contrast to Venezuela's declining influence, Brazil is gaining recognition as the new

leader of Latin America.[119] As Riordan Roett notes,

> Under President Lula's leadership, Brazil has become the most significant
> regional actor in South America—a voice for moderation and integration.
> At the international level, Brazil is now a respected player and interlocutor
> with both the emerging-market countries and the industrialized states.[120]

Brazil's emergence as a regional leader and growing economic power presents the U.S.

with a dilemma; it is at once an important supporter of U.S. regional goals and a

challenge to U.S. regional influence.

Brazil shares the United States' enduring national interests of security,

prosperity, values and international order, although Brasilia does of course have its own

perspective on how to pursue those interests. Although not perfect, Brazil is a stable,

successful democracy and a strong supporter of regional stability. As Hal Brands notes,

> On numerous issues—international trade and finance, energy,
> environmental issues, Security Council reform—Lula has focused less on

undermining the existing order than on increasing Brazil's stake in that order. This strategy has at times led to conflict with the United States... On the whole though, Lula's desire to make Brazil a strong, responsible international stakeholder—as well as Brazil's long land borders, which give Brasilia an immense interest in preserving regional stability—have pushed him toward a foreign policy that, while strongly independent, is largely compatible with U.S. interests.[121]

Lula's pursuit of Brazilian interests has created friction with the U.S. in some specific areas like trade; nevertheless, overall cooperation has increased. As one author noted, "Despite occasional bilateral tensions, the United States and Brazil are cooperating more than ever before in areas including military relations, counternarcotics, energy, and the environment."[122] And as described in a previous section, Brazil is willing to work within the existing international order while seeking reforms to make current structures more equitable for emerging economies. Yet despite the challenges of competition, Brazil is not an economic or ideological threat to the United States – in fact, Brazil is potentially a key future ally.

Nonetheless, Brazil still has hurdles to overcome in its new role as a regional leader. Foremost may be the backlash from its regional neighbors – as one Latin American diplomat quipped, "…the new imperialists have arrived, and they speak Portuguese."[123] Another hurdle will be Brazil's foreign policy inexperience, as Lula's misstep in offering support for Iran so vividly demonstrated. As noted above, Brazil and the U.S. also face challenges in defining the nature and parameters of their new relationship; but both parties have much to gain from increasing cooperation. Skillfully applied, U.S. diplomacy can help Brazil avoid diplomatic blunders and reduce regional backlash. In turn, the U.S. gains a powerful counterpoint to Chavez's radical populism and a regional security partner. The U.S. does not need to counter every Venezuelan initiative or even its ideology; Brazilian leadership and example can help moderate both.

Lula's social development policies and economic model are both successful and sustainable – unlike those adopted by Chavez. Likewise, Brazil's leadership of the MINUSTAH stability mission in Haiti demonstrates that it has become a powerful regional security exporter; a capability that could become critically important in dealing with widespread insecurity inside Venezuela in the aftermath of Chavez's death or removal from power. Chavez's success at fostering anti-Americanism and generating fears of a U.S. invasion over the last fourteen years makes the prospect of a U.S.-led response to a Venezuelan crisis all but impossible. Under such a scenario, Brazilian leadership could be the difference between a relatively permissive stability mission (led by Brazil) and a low intensity quagmire (due to Venezuelan resistance to a U.S.-led mission).

The U.S. has much to gain by viewing Brazil's emergence as the rise of a new regional ally instead of an economic and political threat to U.S. hegemony. Competition is natural between the U.S. and Brazil but cooperation should be the mutual goal. As Abraham Lowenthal notes,

> It is natural that these large and complex countries with such different global positions and different domestic political exigencies will not see eye to eye on every question. But is should be a concern of high priority to negotiate and compromise on matters on which the interests of the two countries are compatible.[124]

The current U.S. administration noted the benefits of Brazilian leadership in its 2011 National Security Strategy when it stated,

> We welcome Brazil's leadership and seek to move beyond dated North-South divisions to pursue progress on bilateral hemispheric, and global issues. Brazil's macroeconomic success, coupled with its steps to narrow socioeconomic gaps, provide important lessons for countries throughout the Americas and Africa.[125]

Nevertheless, much work remains to be done to transform the goal of a robust U.S.-Brazilian partnership into a reality. As the United States enters an era of fiscal constraints and reordered priorities, partnering with Brazil may become more challenging while simultaneously becoming more important to achieving U.S. regional goals.

Conclusion

The election of Hugo Chavez to the presidency of Venezuela in 1998 heralded a new shift to the left in regional politics and generated a competition for the leadership of Latin America. Chavez sought to unify Latin America under the banner of twenty-first century socialism, his personalized form of radical leftist populism (colloquially known as "Chavismo"). Chavez combined personalistic leadership and a polarizing us-against-them political model to implement a socio-economic program that creates dependency in place of development. Chavez's model is highly effective at excluding the political opposition and other rival actors from gaining power, but it is also inherently flawed. Chavismo is anchored on only two pillars—Chavez's personal leadership and oil revenues to fund his system of patronage. Chavez has failed in the race for the leadership of Latin America due in part to his polarizing political style, but mainly because his model is not self-sustaining and cannot be easily replicated in other countries.

With the 2002 election of Luiz Inacio "Lula" da Silva in Brazil, a moderate leftist alternative to Chavez began competing for regional leadership. The Brazilian model rests on the solid foundation of three pillars: diversified economic growth, targeted social development and political inclusion. Brazil's economic diversity generates sustainable growth across a wide range of sectors. This economic growth provides government revenues that fund targeted social development programs. Both of these pillars are supported and reinforced by functioning democratic institutions and a system of political inclusiveness with effective checks and balances. Ten years after Lula's election, the race for the leadership of Latin America is over; and Lula's model won.

The implications for U.S. policy are generally good; radical populism is likely to continue in the region for years to come, but it will not become the dominant political model in Latin America. Likewise, Hugo Chavez and his ALBA supporters will continue to seek to frustrate U.S. regional policy objectives, but Chavez's and ALBA's influence is waning. A more troubling issue on the horizon is the potential for serious internal unrest in Venezuela in the event of Chavez's death or departure from power. Fourteen years of political polarization and the political vacuum triggered by the loss of Chavez are very large obstacles to a peaceful transition of power.

Brazil's emergence as a regional and international power also presents challenges for the United States. It will not be easy for the U.S. to relinquish its historic role as the hegemonic power broker in Latin America. However, Brazil's new leadership role in the region will benefit the U.S. if policymakers and diplomats nurture and mentor Brazil as an emerging regional partner instead of an emerging rival. Brazil shares America's interests in democracy, stability and security. Both parties have vested interests in working together to minimize the negative influences of Chavez and his supporters. Likewise, crafting a regional response – political, economic and military – to a collapse of law and order in Venezuela is another potential area of future bilateral cooperation. Although the U.S. and Brazil will not agree on every issue, each side will reap the benefits of cooperation on issues of shared interest.

Endnotes

[1] Samuel Huntington, *The Third Wave: Democratization in the Late Twentieth Century*, Norman: University of Oklahoma Press, 1991, 25.

[2] Ibid.

[3] Ibid.

[4] Francis Fukuyama, "The 'End of History' 20 Years Later," *New Perspectives Quarterly* 27, no. 1 (Winter 2010): 7.

[5] Francisco Panizza, *Contemporary Latin America: Development and Democracy beyond the Washington Consensus*, (London, Zed Books, 2009), 168; Kurt Weyland, Raúl L. Madrid and Wendy Hunter, eds., *Leftist Governments in Latin America: Successes and Shortcomings*, (New York, Cambridge University Press, 2011), 1; Peruvians elected Ollanta Humala to the presidency in 2011. Coincidently, Humala is also a former army officer who led a failed revolt against Peruvian President Alberto Fujimori in 2000. See http://www.bbc.co.uk/news/world-latin-america-14321996 and
http://www.cnn.com/2011/WORLD/americas/06/06/peru.humala.facts/index.html?iref=allsearch

[6] Sean W. Burges, "Building a Global Southern Coalition: the competing approaches of Brazil's Lula and Venezuela's Chávez," *Third World Quarterly* 28, no. 7 (2007), 1343.

[7] "Contestatory Left:" Weyland, *Leftist Governments*, 3; "Hybrid Regime:"Javier Corrales and Michael Penfold, *Dragon in the Tropics*
Revolution in Venezuela, (Washington, D.C., Brookings Institution Press, 2011), 1; "Neo-populism:" Sebastian Edwards, *Left Behind: Latin America and the False Promise of Populism*, (Chicago, University of Chicago Press, 2010), 192; "Radical Populism:" Hal Brands, "Dealing with political ferment in Latin America: the populist revival, the emergence of the center, and implications for U.S. policy," U.S. Army War College Strategic Studies Institute, 2009, 2.

[8] Panizza, *Contemporary Latin America*, 175.

[9] Edwards, *Left Behind*, 167.

[10] Corrales, *Dragon in the Tropics*, 2-3.

[11] Panizza, *Contemporary Latin America*, 202.

[12] Ibid., 171.

[13] Brands, "Dealing with political ferment," 31.

[14] Gregory Wilpert, *Changing Venezuela by Taking Power*, (London, Verso, 2007), 17.

[15] Ibid., 18.

[16] Panizza, *Contemporary Latin America*, 202. Thirty six percent of Venezuelan voters abstained in the 1998 elections, see Manual Antonio Garretón M. and Edward Newman, eds.,

Democracy in Latin America: (Re)Constructing Political Society, (Tokyo, United Nations University Press, 2001), 152.

[17] Wilpert, *Changing Venezuela*, 13.

[18] Ibid.,12.

[19] George Phillip, *Democracy in Latin America*, (Cambridge, Polity Press, 2003),141-2.

[20] Steve Ellner and Daniel Hellinger, eds., *Venezuelan Politics in the Chávez Era; Class, Polarization and Conflict*, (Boulder, CO, Lynne Rienner Publishers, 2003), 52-3;

[21] Corrales, *Dragon in the Tropics*, 15; Ellner, *Venezuelan Politics*, 85.

[22] Corrales, *Dragon in the Tropics*, 37.

[23] Phillip, *Democracy in Latin America*,134.

[24] Human Rights Watch, "Venezuela: Chavez Allies Pack Supreme Court," December 13, 2004. http://www.hrw.org/print/news/2004/12/13/venezuela-ch-vez-allies-pack-supreme-court (accessed November 25, 2011)

[25] Corrales, *Dragon in the Tropics*, 32.

[26] Ibid.

[27] Javier Corrales, "The Repeating Revolution; Chavez's New Politics and Old Economics," in *Leftist Governments in Latin America: Successes and Shortcomings*, eds. Kurt Weyland, Raúl L. Madrid and Wendy Hunter, (New York, Cambridge University Press, 2011), 30.

[28] Ibid.

[29] World Factbook 2011, Venezuela, https://www.cia.gov/library/publications/the-world-factbook/geos/ve.html (accessed December 10, 2011)

[30] Venezuelanalysis.com, August 5, 2010, "Auditors: Venezuela's State Oil Company Recovering from Oil Price Slump," http://venezuelanalysis.com/print/5554 (accessed December 13, 2011)

[31] Corrales, "The Repeating Revolution," 28.

[32] Ibid.

[33] Wilpert, *Changing Venezuela*, 105.

[34] Ibid., 69.

[35] Francisco Rodriguez, "An Empty Revolution: the Unfulfilled Promises of Hugo Chavez," *Foreign Relations* 87, no. 2 (Mar/Apr 2008), 2.

[36] Panizza, *Contemporary Latin America,* 206.

[37] Ibid.

[38] Rodriguez, "An Empty Revolution," 2.

[39] Ibid.

[40] Ibid.

[41] Corrales, "The Repeating Revolution," 45.

[42] Wilpert, *Changing Venezuela*, 192.

[43] Ibid., 193.

[44] Corrales, *Dragon in the Tropics*, 42.

[45] Ibid., 42-3.

[46] Wilpert, *Changing Venezuela*, 152.

[47] Corrales, *Dragon in the Tropics*, 101.

[48] Ibid., 102.

[49] Ibid., 103.

[50] Ibid., 104.

[51] Ibid., 104-7; Sean W. Burges, "Building a Global Southern Coalition: the competing approaches of Brazil's Lula and Venezuela's Chávez," *Third World Quarterly* 28, no. 7 (2007), 1348.

[52] Brands, "Dealing with political ferment," 11.

[53] Corrales, *Dragon in the Tropics*, 108.

[54] Ibid., 107.

[55] Ibid., 109.

[56] Ibid., 114.

[57] Edwards, *Left Behind,* 210.

[58] Peter R. Kingstone and Aldo F. Ponce, "From Cardoso to Lula; The Triumph of Pragmatism in Brazil," in *Leftist Governments in Latin America: Successes and Shortcomings,*

eds. Kurt Weyland, Raúl L. Madrid and Wendy Hunter, (New York, Cambridge University Press, 2011), 102-3.

[59] Wendy Hunter, *The Transformation of the Workers' Party in Brazil, 1989-2009*, (New York, Cambridge University Press, 2010), 146.

[60] Edwards, *Left Behind,* 205.

[61] Kingstone and Ponce, "From Cardoso to Lula," 98.

[62] Panizza, *Contemporary Latin America,* 212.

[63] Ibid., 213.

[64] Kingstone and Ponce, "From Cardoso to Lula," 102-3.

[65] CIA World Factbook, accessed at https://www.cia.gov/library/publications/the-world-factbook/geos/br.html (accessed December 17, 2011)

[66] Edwards, *Left Behind,* 205.

[67] Kingstone and Ponce, "From Cardoso to Lula," 99.

[68] Ibid.

[69] Ibid.

[70] Hunter, *Workers' Party in Brazil,* 149.

[71] Kingstone and Ponce, "From Cardoso to Lula," 112.

[72] Ibid., 113.

[73] Hunter, *Workers' Party in Brazil,* 154.

[74] Ibid., 154.

[75] Edwards, *Left Behind,* 211; Hunter, *Workers' Party in Brazil,* 154.

[76] Edwards, *Left Behind,* 212.

[77] Kingstone and Ponce, "From Cardoso to Lula," 117.

[78] Edwards, *Left Behind,* 212.

[79] Hunter, *Workers' Party in Brazil,* 155.

[80] Edwards, *Left Behind,* 211.

[81] Kingstone and Ponce, "From Cardoso to Lula," 112.

[82] Ibid.

[83] Edwards, *Left Behind,* 212.

[84] Kingstone and Ponce, "From Cardoso to Lula," 120.

[85] Ibid.

[86] Ibid.

[87] Hunter, *Workers' Party in Brazil,* 157-8.

[88] Riordan Roett, *The New Brazil*, (Washington, D.C., Brookings Institution Press, 2010), 130.

[89] Ibid.

[90] Julia Sweig, "A New Global Player: Brazil's Far Flung Agenda," *Foreign Affairs* 89, no. 6 (Nov/Dec 2010), 6.

[91] Hunter, *Workers' Party in Brazil,* 157; Burges, "Building a Global Southern Coalition," 1351.

[92] Roett, *The New Brazil*, 4.

[93] UPI online, "Brazil campaigning for permanent U.N. Security Council seat" http://www.upi.com/Top_News/Special/2009/10/16/Brazil-campaigning-for-permanent-UN-Security-Council-seat/UPI-71131255711794/ (accessed November 12, 2011); Burges, "Building a Global Southern Coalition," 1352.

[94] United Nations Security Council report, February 2006, Haiti MINUSTAH, http://www.securitycouncilreport.org/site/pp.aspx?c=glKWLeMTIsG&b=1387811&printmode=1 (accessed December 18, 2011)

[95] Sweig, "A New Global Player," 2; UN Department of Peacekeeping Operations http://www.un.org/en/peacekeeping/missions/minustah/ (accessed December 22, 2011); United Nations Security Council report, February 2006, Haiti MINUSTAH http://www.securitycouncilreport.org/site/pp.aspx?c=glKWLeMTIsG&b=1387811&printmode=1 (accessed December 22, 2011)

[96] Roett, *The New Brazil*, 146.

[97] Ibid.,147; Alexei Barrionuevo and Ginger Thompson, "Brazil's Iran Diplomacy Worries U.S. Officials," *The New York Times*, May 14, 2010. http://www.nytimes.com/2010/05/15/world/americas/15lula.html (accessed February 4, 2012)

[98] Sweig, "A New Global Player," 3.

[99] Roett, *The New Brazil*, 147.

[100] STRATFOR, "Brazil and Iran: An Unlikely Partnership," November 24, 2009, 2.

[101] Sweig, "A New Global Player," 4.

[102] Guy Taylor, The Washington Times, http://www.washingtontimes.com/news/2012/jan/7/us-eyeing-iranian-leaders-trip-to-latin-america/ (accessed December 22, 2011)

[103] Brands, "Dealing with political ferment," 17.

[104] Russell Crandall, "The Post-American Hemisphere: Power and Politics in an Autonomous Latin America," *Foreign Affairs* 90, no. 3, (May/Jun 2011): 2.

[105] Corrales, *Dragon in the Tropics*, 135.

[106] Burges, "Building a Global Southern Coalition," 1355.

[107] Corrales, *Dragon in the Tropics*, 131.

[108] STRATFOR, "The Obama Administration and Latin America," February 11, 2009, 4.

[109] STRATFOR, "The United States and the 'Problem' of Venezuela," February 22, 2006, 3.

[110] Oil exports did virtually cease during the nation-wide general strike from December 2, 2002, until February 2, 2003. However, the disruption was due to a strike in opposition to Chavez and not a decision by him to cut off oil exports. See United States Government Accountability Office report "Energy Security: Issues Related to Potential Reductions in Venezuelan Oil Production," June 2006 http://www.gao.gov/new.items/d06668.pdf (accessed December 22, 2011)

[111] Corrales, *Dragon in the Tropics*, 116, 117.

[112] Ibid., 116.

[113] Rodriguez, "An Empty Revolution," 5.

[114] STRATFOR, "Venezuela: Tough Choices Ahead," January 7, 2009, 1.

[115] Wilpert, *Changing Venezuela*, 13.

[116] CNN online, "Chavez still battling cancer, Spanish newspaper says," http://www.cnn.com/2012/01/23/world/americas/venezuela-chavez-health/index.html (accessed January 24, 2012)

[117] STRATFOR, "Prospects for a Post-Chavez-Venezuela," July 5, 2011, 1.

[118] Author's personal analysis based on thirteen years experience as a Latin American Foreign Area Officer, including over three years serving as a Latin American political-military analyst with the Defense Intelligence Agency.

[119] Roett, *The New Brazil*, 132; Crandall, "The Post-American Hemisphere," 1; Burges, "Building a Global Southern Coalition," 1355; Sweig, "A New Global Player," 1.

[120] Roett, *The New Brazil*, 152.

[121] Brands, "Dealing with political ferment," 38.

[122] Crandall, "The Post-American Hemisphere," 5.

[123] Ibid., 3.

[124] Abraham Lowenthal, "Obama and the Americas," *Foreign Affairs* 89, no. 4 (Jul/Aug 2010), 1.

[125] Barrack Obama, *National Security Strategy*, (Washington, DC: The White House, May 2010), 44.